simply

vegetarian

simply
vegetarian

100 no fuss recipes for everyday cooking

First published in 2012
LOVE FOOD is an imprint of Parragon Books Ltd

Parragon
Chartist House
15-17 Trim Street
Bath BA1 1HA, UK

ISBN: 978-1-4454-3765-1

Printed in China

Introduction by Linda Doeser
New recipes and cover food styling by Teresa Goldfinch
Cover photography by Clive Streeter
Additional photography by Clive Bozzard-Hill
Additional food styling by Val Barrett

Notes for the Reader
This book uses imperial, metric, and US cup measurements.
Follow the same units of measurement throughout; do not mix
imperial and metric. All spoon measurements are level: teaspoons
are assumed to be 5 ml, and tablespoons are assumed to be
15 ml. Unless otherwise stated, milk is assumed to be whole, eggs
are large, individual vegetables, such as potatoes, are medium, and
pepper is freshly ground black pepper.

The times given are an approximate guide only. Preparation times
differ according to the techniques used by different people and
the cooking times may also vary from those given as a result of
the type of oven used. Optional ingredients, variations, or serving
suggestions have not been included in the calculations.

Recipes using raw or very lightly cooked eggs should be avoided
by infants, the elderly, pregnant women, convalescents, and anyone
with a chronic condition. Pregnant and breast-feeding women are
advised to avoid eating peanuts and peanut products. People with
nut allergies should be aware that some of the prepared ingredients
used in the recipes in this book may contain nuts. Always check the
package before use.

Vegetarians should be aware that some of the prepared
ingredients used in the recipes in this book may contain animal
products. Always check the package before use.

Contents

Introduction

In the last two or three decades, increasing numbers of people have turned to a vegetarian diet. As a result, recipes for vegetarian dishes, once heavily dependent on beans, pasta, and cheese, have become wonderfully varied and innovative. This period also coincided with exponential growth in international travel that provided the opportunity for people to explore the cuisines of many other cultures, including those with a long-standing vegetarian tradition, such as the Indian subcontinent and Southeast Asia. The vacation destinations of southern Europe and the Mediterranean have also offered inspiration because, although their cuisines are by no means vegetarian, they feature a vast array of superb vegetable dishes.

In fact, vegetarian dishes have become so mainstream that they play a major role on the menus of exclusive restaurants in towns and cities throughout the country. Even nonvegetarians relish such delicious treats as warm goat cheese salad and caramelized onion tart, not because they are vegetarian or are thought to be healthy, but because they look so appetizing and taste so delectable.

Like any diet, a vegetarian one can be good or bad and it may surprise some people to learn that vegetarian dishes are not automatically healthy, although it is certainly true that the Western diet tends to include unhealthy amounts of meat, animal products, and saturated fats. It is equally true that a diet that contains a high proportion of vegetables, including beans and other legumes, is good for the heart and digestive system, helps protect against a number of diseases, and is rich in vitamins and many minerals. It is easier for meat eaters to obtain enough protein because animal products contain all the essential amino acids, the building blocks of proteins. Virtually no vegetarian ingredient contains all these essential amino acids, but many contain some of them—nuts, beans, grains, tofu, eggs, cheese, and other dairy products. Combining these different ingredients guarantees that a meal contains what is known as complete protein. This often happens automatically so, for example, a vegetarian chili containing kidney beans will usually be served on a bed of rice, and this combination of beans and grain contains all the essential amino acids.

However, rather than worrying about whether there is a balance of nuts or dairy products, the simplest way to make sure that a vegetarian diet is healthy is to make it as varied as possible.

Top Tips for Success

• Always check the labels on products when shopping to avoid inadvertently buying animal products. Regular Worcestershire sauce, for example, contains anchovies, but a vegetarian version is available. Some block margarines contain fish oils, while some low-fat spreads include gelatin. Labels will also identify brands fortified with vitamins, such as B12 and D, and this can be important for vegans and vegetarians who eat few dairy products. Some soft cheeses, such as ricotta, cream cheese, and farmer's cheese, don't usually contain rennet, an animal enzyme used in the production of harder cheeses, but check the label before buying.

• Buy vegetables and fruit in peak condition, preferably locally grown and seasonal, because lengthy transportation depletes the vitamin content. Store vegetables in a cool, dark place and don't leave them standing or soaking in water for a long time after preparing them.

• Buy spices in small quantities and store them in a cool, dark place because they quickly lose their aroma and flavor. For the best flavor, buy whole spices and grind them yourself.

• Buy nuts and seeds in small quantities because they quickly become rancid because of their high oil content.

• Store beans and lentils in an airtight container in a cool, dark place. Make a note of the expiration date, because after about six months, the skins become tough and they require much longer cooking. When using canned beans, drain and rinse them to remove any sugar and/or salt used in processing.

• Store tofu in the refrigerator. Once opened, it will keep for up to a week in a bowl of cold water in the refrigerator; change the water daily.

• Iron is a particularly important mineral for teenage girls and young women, but the human body is less efficient at absorbing it from vegetable than from animal sources. When serving iron-rich foods—dark green leafy vegetables, tofu, and beans—include something rich in vitamin C at the same meal, because this increases the uptake. Avoid drinking tea at the meal because tannin decreases the uptake.

• Too much fat, especially saturated fat, is not good in any diet, vegetarian or otherwise. Eggs, cheese, cream, and some other dairy products have a high fat content and should be used sparingly. Look for low-fat or reduced-fat alternatives. Low-fat and skim milk have the same nutritional value as whole.

Super Soups & Appetizers

creamy tomato & basil soup

SERVES 6

2 tbsp butter

1 tbsp olive oil

1 onion, finely chopped

1 garlic clove, chopped

2 lb/900 g plum tomatoes, chopped

2¾ cups vegetable stock

½ cup dry white wine

2 tbsp sun-dried tomato paste

2 tbsp torn fresh basil leaves, plus extra to garnish

⅔ cup heavy cream

salt and pepper

1 Melt the butter with the oil in a large, heavy-bottom pan. Add the onion and cook, stirring occasionally, for 5 minutes, or until softened. Add the garlic, tomatoes, stock, wine, and tomato paste, stir well, and season to taste. Partially cover the pan and simmer, stirring occasionally, for 20–25 minutes, or until the mixture is soft and pulpy.

2 Remove the pan from the heat, let cool slightly, then pour into a blender or food processor. Add the torn basil and process. Push the mixture through a strainer into a clean pan with a wooden spoon.

3 Stir in the cream and reheat the soup, but do not let it boil. Ladle the soup into warm bowls, garnish with the basil leaves, and serve immediately.

mixed bean soup

SERVES 4

1 medium onion, chopped

**1 garlic clove,
finely chopped**

2 celery stalks, sliced

1 large carrot, diced

**14 oz/400 g canned
chopped tomatoes**

⅔ cup red wine

5 cups vegetable stock

1 tsp dried oregano

**15 oz/425 g canned mixed
beans and legumes**

2 medium zucchini, diced

1 tbsp tomato paste

salt and pepper

**store-bought pesto,
to garnish**

1 Place the onion, garlic, celery, and carrot in a large pan. Stir in the tomatoes, red wine, vegetable stock, and oregano. Bring the vegetable mixture to a boil, cover, and simmer for 15 minutes.

2 Stir the beans and zucchini into the mixture and continue to cook, uncovered, for an additional 5 minutes. Add the tomato paste to the mixture and season well with salt and pepper to taste.

3 Heat through, stirring occasionally, for an additional 2–3 minutes, but do not let the mixture boil again. Ladle the soup into warm bowls and serve, garnished with a spoonful of pesto.

watercress soup

SERVES 4

2 bunches of watercress (about 7 oz/200 g), thoroughly cleaned

3 tbsp butter

2 onions, chopped

1½ cups coarsely chopped potatoes

5 cups vegetable stock or water

salt and pepper

whole nutmeg, for grating (optional)

½ cup sour cream, to serve

1 Remove the leaves from the stalks of the watercress and keep on one side. Roughly chop the stalks.

2 Melt the butter in a large pan over medium heat, add the onion, and cook for 4–5 minutes, until soft. Do not brown.

3 Add the potato to the pan and mix well with the onion. Add the watercress stalks and the stock. Bring to a boil, then reduce the heat, cover, and simmer for 15–20 minutes, until the potato is soft.

4 Add the watercress leaves and stir in to heat through. Remove from the heat and use a handheld immersion blender to process the soup until smooth. Alternatively, pour the soup into a blender, process until smooth, and return to the rinsed-out pan.

5 Reheat and season with salt and pepper, adding a good grating of nutmeg, if using. Ladle into warm bowls and serve with sour cream spooned on top.

vegetable & corn chowder

SERVES 4

1 tbsp vegetable oil

1 red onion, diced

1 red bell pepper, seeded and diced

3 garlic cloves, crushed

1¾ cups diced potatoes

2 tbsp all-purpose flour

2½ cups milk

1¼ cups vegetable stock

½ cup broccoli florets

3 cups drained canned corn kernels

¾ cup grated cheddar cheese

salt and pepper

1 Heat the oil in a large pan. Add the onion, bell pepper, garlic, and potatoes and sauté over low heat, stirring frequently, for 2–3 minutes.

2 Stir in the flour and cook, stirring for 30 seconds. Gradually stir in the milk and stock.

3 Add the broccoli and corn kernels. Bring the mixture to a boil, stirring continuously, then reduce the heat and simmer for about 20 minutes, or until all the vegetables are tender. Add ½ cup of the cheese and stir until it melts.

4 Season to taste and ladle into warm bowls. Garnish with the remaining cheese and serve.

Step 1

Step 2

Step 3

borscht

SERVES 6

1 onion

4 tbsp butter

**12 oz/350 g beets,
cut into thin sticks,
and 1 beet, grated**

1 carrot, cut into thin sticks

**3 celery stalks,
thinly sliced**

**2 tomatoes, peeled,
seeded, and chopped**

6¼ cups vegetable stock

1 tbsp white wine vinegar

1 tbsp sugar

**2 large sprigs fresh dill,
plus extra to garnish**

**1¼ cups shredded
white cabbage**

salt and pepper

**⅔ cup sour cream,
to garnish**

1 Slice the onion into rings. Melt the butter in a large, heavy-bottom pan. Add the onion and cook over low heat, stirring occasionally, for 3–5 minutes, or until softened. Add the sticks of beet, the carrot, celery, and chopped tomatoes and cook, stirring frequently, for 4–5 minutes.

2 Add the stock, vinegar, and sugar and snip a tablespoon of dill into the pan. Season to taste with salt and pepper. Bring to a boil, reduce the heat, and simmer for 35–40 minutes, or until the vegetables are tender.

3 Stir in the cabbage, cover, and simmer for 10 minutes, then stir in the grated beet, with any juices, and cook for an additional 10 minutes. Ladle the borscht into warm bowls. Garnish with sour cream and another tablespoon of snipped dill, and serve.

carrot & cumin soup

SERVES 4–6

3 tbsp butter or margarine

1 large onion, chopped

1–2 garlic cloves, crushed

3 cups sliced carrots

3¾ cups vegetable stock

¾ tsp ground cumin

2 celery stalks, thinly sliced

1 cup diced potato

2 tsp tomato paste

2 tsp lemon juice

2 fresh or dried bay leaves

generous 1¼ cups low-fat milk

salt and pepper

celery leaves, to garnish

1 Melt the butter or margarine in a large pan. Add the onion and garlic and cook very gently until softened.

2 Add the carrots and cook gently for an additional 5 minutes, stirring frequently and be careful they do not brown.

3 Add the stock, cumin, celery, potato, tomato paste, lemon juice, and bay leaves and bring to a boil. Season to taste with salt and pepper. Cover and simmer for about 30 minutes until the vegetables are tender.

4 Remove and discard the bay leaves, cool the soup a little, and then press it through a strainer or process in a food processor or blender until smooth.

5 Pour the soup into a clean pan, add the milk, and bring to a boil over low heat. Taste and adjust the seasoning, if necessary. Ladle into warm bowls, garnish each serving with a small celery leaf and serve.

bell pepper & chile soup

SERVES 4

2 red bell peppers, seeded and sliced

1 onion, sliced

2 garlic cloves, crushed

1 green chile, chopped

1¼ cups strained pureed tomatoes

2½ cups vegetable stock

2 tbsp chopped basil, plus extra to garnish

1 Put the red bell peppers in a large pan with the onion, garlic, and chile. Add the strained tomatoes and the vegetable stock and bring to a boil, stirring well.

2 Reduce the heat to a simmer and continue to cook the vegetables for 20 minutes, or until the bell peppers are soft. Drain, reserving the liquid and vegetables separately.

3 Using the back of a spoon, press the vegetables through a strainer. Alternatively, process in a food processor until smooth.

4 Return the vegetable puree to a clean pan with the reserved cooking liquid. Add the basil and heat through until hot. Ladle into warm bowls, garnish with basil, and serve immediately.

white bean soup

SERVES 4

**scant 1 cup dried cannellini
beans, soaked in cold
water overnight**

6 cups vegetable stock

**4 oz/115 g dried corallini,
conchigliette piccole,
or other soup pasta**

6 tbsp olive oil

**2 garlic cloves,
finely chopped**

**4 tbsp chopped fresh
flat-leaf parsley**

salt and pepper

fresh crusty bread, to serve

1 Drain the soaked beans and place them in a large, heavy-bottom pan. Add the stock and bring to a boil. Partially cover the pan, then reduce the heat and let simmer for 2 hours, or until tender.

2 Transfer about half of the beans and a little of the stock to a food processor or blender and process to a smooth puree. Return the puree to the pan and stir well to mix. Return the soup to a boil.

3 Add the pasta to the soup, return to a boil, and cook for 10 minutes, or until tender.

4 Meanwhile, heat 4 tablespoons of the olive oil in a small pan. Add the garlic and cook over low heat, stirring frequently, for 4–5 minutes, or until golden. Stir the garlic into the soup and add the parsley. Season with salt and pepper and ladle into warm soup bowls. Drizzle with the remaining olive oil and serve immediately with crusty bread.

Step
1

Step
2

Step
3

lettuce & arugula soup

SERVES 4–6

1 tbsp butter

1 large onion, halved and sliced

2 leeks, sliced

6¼ cups vegetable stock

6 tbsp white rice

2 carrots, thinly sliced

3 garlic cloves

1 bay leaf

2 heads soft round lettuce (about 1 lb/450 g), cored and chopped

¾ cup heavy cream, plus extra to garnish

freshly grated nutmeg

3⅔ cups finely chopped arugula leaves

salt and pepper

1 Heat the butter in a large pan over medium heat and add the onion and leeks. Cover and cook for 3–4 minutes, stirring frequently, until the vegetables begin to soften.

2 Add the stock, rice, carrots, garlic, and bay leaf with a large pinch of salt. Bring just to a boil. Reduce the heat, cover, and simmer for 25–30 minutes, or until the rice and vegetables are tender. Remove and discard the bay leaf.

3 Add the lettuce and cook for 10 minutes, until the leaves are softened, stirring occasionally.

4 Let the soup cool slightly, then transfer to a blender or food processor and puree until smooth, working in batches if necessary. (If using a food processor, strain off the cooking liquid and reserve. Puree the soup solids with enough cooking liquid to moisten them, then combine with the remaining liquid.)

5 Return the soup to the pan and place over medium–low heat. Stir in the cream and a grating of nutmeg. Simmer gently for about 5 minutes, stirring occasionally, until the soup is reheated. Add more water or cream if you prefer a thinner soup.

6 Add the arugula and ladle the soup into warm bowls. Garnish with cream and arugula and serve immediately.

creamed mushrooms

SERVES 4

juice of 1 small lemon

1 lb/450 g small button mushrooms

2 tbsp butter

1 tbsp sunflower or olive oil

1 small onion, finely chopped

½ cup heavy cream

1 tbsp chopped fresh parsley, plus 4 sprigs to garnish

salt and pepper

1 Sprinkle a little of the lemon juice over the mushrooms. Heat the butter and oil in a skillet, add the onion, and cook for 1 minute. Add the mushrooms, shaking the skillet so they do not stick.

2 Season with salt and pepper, then stir in the cream, chopped parsley, and remaining lemon juice.

3 Heat until hot but don't let boil, then transfer to a serving plate and garnish with the parsley sprigs. Serve immediately.

hot garlic-stuffed mushrooms

SERVES 4

4 large portobello mushrooms

4 sprays olive oil

2–3 garlic cloves, crushed

2 shallots

½ cup fresh whole wheat breadcrumbs

few fresh basil sprigs

scant ¼ cup chopped plumped dried apricots

1 tbsp pine nuts

2 oz/55 g feta cheese

1 Preheat the oven to 350°F/180°C. Remove the stalks from the mushrooms and set aside. Spray the bottoms of the mushrooms with the oil and place undersides up in a roasting pan.

2 Put the mushroom stalks in a food processor with the garlic, shallots, and breadcrumbs. Set aside a few basil sprigs for the garnish, then place the remainder in the food processor with the apricots, pine nuts, and feta cheese.

3 Process for 1–2 minutes, or until a stuffing consistency is formed, then divide among the mushroom caps.

4 Bake for 10–12 minutes, or until the mushrooms are tender and the stuffing is crisp on the top. Serve garnished with the reserved basil sprigs.

mini roasted vegetable skewers

SERVES 4

1 red bell pepper, seeded

1 yellow bell pepper, seeded

1 large zucchini

1 eggplant

2 tbsp olive oil

3 garlic cloves, crushed

salt and pepper

dip

2 tbsp chopped fresh dill

2 tbsp chopped fresh mint

generous 1 cup plain yogurt

1 Preheat the oven to 400°F/200°C. Cut the vegetables into ¾-inch/2-cm chunks. Put them into a roasting pan large enough to hold them in a single layer.

2 Combine the olive oil and garlic and drizzle over the top. Season well with salt and pepper, then toss together. Roast for 25–30 minutes, until tender and lightly charred.

3 Meanwhile, stir the dill and mint into the yogurt. Spoon into 4 serving bowls.

4 When the vegetables are cool enough to handle, divide them among 12 wooden toothpicks. Serve warm or cold with the bowls of dip on the side.

Step 1

Step 2

Step 3

vegetable tartlets

MAKES 12

butter, for greasing

12 prepared individual pastry shells

2 tbsp olive oil

1 red bell pepper, seeded and diced

1 garlic clove, crushed

1 small onion, finely chopped

1¼ cups chopped ripe tomatoes

1 tbsp torn fresh basil

1 tsp fresh or dried thyme

salt and pepper

green salad, to serve

1 Preheat the oven to 400°F/200°C and grease several baking sheets. Place the ready-baked pastry shells on the baking sheets.

2 Heat the oil in a skillet, add the bell pepper, garlic, and onion, and cook over high heat for about 3 minutes, until soft.

3 Add the tomatoes, herbs, and salt and pepper and spoon onto the pastry shells.

4 Bake for about 5 minutes, or until the filling is piping hot. Serve warm with a green salad.

hummus

SERVES 8

generous 1 cup dried chickpeas, covered with water and soaked overnight

juice of 2 large lemons

⅔ cup tahini paste

2 garlic cloves, crushed

4 tbsp extra virgin olive oil

small pinch of ground cumin

1 tsp paprika

1 tbsp chopped fresh flat-leaf parsley

salt and pepper

warm pita bread, to serve

1 Drain the chickpeas, place in a saucepan, and cover with cold water. Bring to a boil, then simmer for about 2 hours, until very tender.

2 Drain the chickpeas, reserving a little of the liquid, and put in a food processor or blender, reserving a few to garnish. Blend the chickpeas until smooth, gradually adding the lemon juice and enough reserved liquid to form a smooth, thick paste. Add the tahini paste, garlic, 3 tablespoons of the oil, and the cumin and blend until smooth. Season to taste with salt and pepper.

3 Turn the mixture into a shallow serving dish and chill in the refrigerator for 2–3 hours before serving. To serve, mix the remaining oil with the paprika and drizzle over the top of the dish. Sprinkle with the parsley and the reserved chickpeas. Serve immediately, accompanied by warm pita bread.

mushroom pâté

SERVES 4

scant ¼ cup dried porcini mushrooms

1 tsp olive oil

2 shallots, finely chopped

2 garlic cloves, crushed

1 fresh jalapeño chile, seeded and finely chopped

2 celery stalks, trimmed and finely chopped

3¼ cups wiped and sliced button mushrooms

grated rind and juice of 1 orange

½ cup fresh breadcrumbs

1 tbsp chopped fresh parsley

1 small egg, beaten

pepper

raw vegetable sticks and crispbreads, to serve

1 Preheat the oven to 350°F/180°C. Put the dried mushrooms in a bowl and cover with freshly boiled water. Let soak for 30 minutes, then drain, chop, and set aside.

2 Heat the oil in a medium heavy-bottom pan, then add the shallots, garlic, chile, and celery. Cook, stirring frequently, for 3 minutes, then add both the dried and fresh mushrooms and cook for an additional 2 minutes.

3 Add the orange juice and continue to cook for 3–4 minutes, or until the mushrooms have collapsed. Remove the pan from the heat and stir in the orange rind, breadcrumbs, parsley, beaten egg, and pepper to taste. Mix well.

4 Spoon the mixture into 4 individual ramekin dishes and level the surfaces. Place the dishes in a small baking pan and pour enough water to come halfway up the sides of the ramekins.

5 Cook for 15–20 minutes, or until a skewer inserted in the center of each ramekin comes out clean. Remove and either let stand for 10 minutes before serving warm or chill until ready to serve. Turn out and serve with vegetable sticks and crispbreads.

eggplant pâté

SERVES 4–6

2 large eggplants

4 tbsp extra virgin olive oil

**2 garlic cloves,
very finely chopped**

4 tbsp lemon juice

salt and pepper

**2 tbsp coarsely chopped
fresh flat-leaf parsley,
to garnish**

6 crispbreads, to serve

1 Preheat the oven to 350°F/180°C. Score the skins of the eggplants with the point of a sharp knife, without piercing the flesh, and place them on a baking sheet. Bake for 1¼ hours, or until soft.

2 Remove the eggplants from the oven and let stand until cool enough to handle. Cut them in half and, using a spoon, scoop out the flesh into a bowl. Mash the flesh thoroughly.

3 Gradually beat in the olive oil, then stir in the garlic and lemon juice. Season with salt and pepper to taste. Cover with plastic wrap and store in the refrigerator until required. Garnish with parsley and serve with crispbreads.

Step
1

Step
2

Step
3

stuffed eggplant slices

SERVES 4

1 medium eggplant

4 tbsp extra virgin olive oil

1 cup grated mozzarella cheese

1 tbsp chopped fresh basil, plus extra leaves to garnish

14 oz/400 g canned chopped tomatoes with added herbs

1 Preheat the oven to 400°F/200°C. Slice the eggplant lengthwise into 8 slices. Brush the slices with oil and place on a baking sheet. Bake for 10 minutes, without letting them get too floppy. Remove from the oven. Sprinkle the grated cheese and basil over the eggplant slices.

2 Roll up each slice and place the slices in a single layer in a shallow ovenproof dish. Pour the chopped tomatoes over them and cook in the oven for 10 minutes, or until the sauce bubbles and the cheese melts.

3 Remove the stuffed eggplant slices from the oven and transfer carefully to serving plates. Spoon any remaining chopped tomatoes on or around the eggplant slices. Garnish with basil leaves and serve while still hot.

quesadillas

SERVES 4

4 tbsp finely chopped fresh jalapeño chiles

1 onion, chopped

1 tbsp red wine vinegar

5 tbsp extra virgin olive oil

10½–14 oz/300–400 g canned corn kernels

8 soft flour tortillas

1 Put the chiles, onion, vinegar, and 4 tablespoons of olive oil in a food processor and process until finely chopped. Turn into a bowl and stir in the corn.

2 Heat the remaining oil in a skillet, add a tortilla, and cook for 1 minute, until golden. Spread some of the chile mixture over the tortilla and fold over.

3 Cook for 2–3 minutes, until golden and the filling is heated through. Remove from the skillet and keep warm. Repeat with the other tortillas and filling. Serve immediately.

egg rolls

MAKES 12

**5 dried Chinese
mushrooms or fresh
open-cap mushrooms**

1 large carrot

**2 oz/55 g canned bamboo
shoots**

**2 scallions, trimmed,
plus a few more to
garnish**

2 oz/55 g napa cabbage

**2 tbsp vegetable oil,
plus extra for
deep-frying**

**generous 2 cups bean
sprouts**

1 tbsp soy sauce

12 egg roll wrappers

1 egg, beaten

salt

1 Place the mushrooms in a small bowl and cover with warm water. Let soak for 20–25 minutes, then drain and squeeze out the excess water. Remove the coarse centers and slice the mushroom caps thinly. Cut the carrot and bamboo shoots into very thin julienne strips. Chop the 2 scallions and shred the napa cabbage.

2 Heat 2 tablespoons of oil in a preheated wok. Add the mushrooms, carrot, and bamboo shoots and stir-fry for 2 minutes. Add the scallions, napa cabbage, bean sprouts, and soy sauce. Season to taste with salt and stir-fry for 2 minutes. Cool.

3 Divide the mixture into 12 equal portions and place 1 portion on the edge of each egg roll wrapper. Fold in the sides and roll each one up, brushing the seam with beaten egg to seal. Heat the oil for deep-frying in a large, heavy-bottom pan to 350–375°F/180–190°C, or until a cube of bread browns in 30 seconds. Add the egg rolls, in batches, and cook for 4–5 minutes, or until golden and crispy. Be careful that the oil is not too hot or the rolls will brown on the outside before cooking on the inside. Drain on paper towels. Keep warm. Garnish with the scallions and serve.

roasted vegetable & feta wraps

MAKES 4

1 red onion, cut into eighths

1 red bell pepper, seeded and cut into eighths

1 small eggplant, cut into eighths

1 zucchini, cut into eighths

4 tbsp extra-virgin olive oil

1 garlic clove, crushed

⅔ cup crumbled feta cheese

small bunch of fresh mint, shredded

4 sun-dried tomato wraps, 10 inches/25 cm each

salt and pepper

1 Preheat the oven to 425°F/220°C. Mix the vegetables, olive oil, garlic, and some salt and pepper together and place in the oven in a nonstick roasting pan. Cook for 15–20 minutes, or until golden and cooked through.

2 Remove from the oven and let cool. Mix in the cheese and mint.

3 Preheat a nonstick skillet or broiler pan until almost smoking, add the wraps, 1 at a time, and cook for 10 seconds on each side. This will add some color and soften the wraps.

4 Divide the vegetable-and-cheese mixture evenly among the wraps, placing some along the center of each wrap. Fold in each wrap at the ends, roll up, cut in half, and serve.

Step 1

Step 2

Step 4

phyllo-wrapped asparagus

SERVES 4

dip

⅓ cup cottage cheese

1 tbsp low-fat milk

4 scallions, trimmed and finely chopped

2 tbsp chopped fresh mixed herbs, such as basil, mint, and tarragon

pepper

asparagus

20 asparagus spears

5 sheets phyllo dough

lemon wedges, to serve

1 Preheat the oven to 375°F/190°C. To make the dip, put the cottage cheese in a bowl and add the milk. Beat until smooth, then stir in the scallions, chopped herbs, and pepper to taste. Place in a serving bowl, cover lightly, and chill in the refrigerator until required.

2 Cut off and discard the woody end of the asparagus and shave with a vegetable peeler to remove any woody parts from the spears.

3 Cut the phyllo dough into quarters and place one sheet on a clean surface. Brush lightly with water, then place a spear at one end. Roll up to encase the spear, and place on a large baking sheet. Repeat until all the asparagus spears are wrapped in dough.

4 Bake for 10–12 minutes, or until the pastry is golden. Serve the spears with lemon wedges and the dip on the side.

bell pepper & basil stacks

SERVES 4

1 tsp olive oil

2 shallots, finely chopped

2 garlic cloves, crushed

2 red bell peppers, peeled, seeded, and sliced into strips

1 orange bell pepper, peeled, seeded, and sliced into strips

4 tomatoes, thinly sliced

2 tbsp shredded fresh basil

pepper

salad greens, to serve

1 Lightly brush 4 ramekin dishes with the oil. Mix the shallots and garlic together in a bowl and season with pepper to taste.

2 Layer the red and orange bell peppers with the tomatoes in the prepared ramekin dishes, sprinkling each layer with the shallot mixture and shredded basil. When all the ingredients have been added, cover lightly with plastic wrap or parchment paper. Weigh down using small weights and let stand in the refrigerator for at least 6 hours, or preferably overnight.

3 When ready to serve, remove the weights and carefully run a knife around the edges. Invert onto serving plates and serve with salad greens.

tomato bruschetta

SERVES 4

8 slices rustic bread

4 garlic cloves, halved

8 plum tomatoes, peeled and diced

extra virgin olive oil, for drizzling

salt and pepper

fresh basil leaves, to garnish

1 Preheat the broiler. Lightly toast the bread on both sides. Rub each piece of toast with half of a garlic clove and then return to the broiler for a few seconds.

2 Divide the diced tomatoes among the toasts. Season with salt and pepper to taste and drizzle with olive oil. Serve immediately, garnished with basil leaves.

wild mushroom bruschetta

SERVES 4

4 slices sourdough bread, such as Pugliese

3 garlic cloves, 1 halved and 2 crushed

2 tbsp extra virgin olive oil

8 oz/225 g mixed wild mushrooms, such as porcini, chanterelles, and portobello mushrooms

1 tbsp olive oil

2 tbsp butter

1 small onion or 2 shallots, finely chopped

¼ cup dry white wine or Marsala

salt and pepper

2 tbsp coarsely chopped fresh flat-leaf parsley, to garnish

1 Toast the bread slices under a preheated broiler or in a preheated ridged grill pan on both sides, then rub with the garlic halves and drizzle with the extra virgin olive oil. Transfer to a baking sheet and keep warm in a warm oven.

2 Wipe the mushrooms thoroughly to remove any trace of soil, and slice any large ones. Heat the olive oil with half of the butter in a skillet, then add the mushrooms and cook over medium heat, stirring frequently, for 3–4 minutes, or until soft. Remove with a slotted spoon and keep warm in the oven.

3 Heat the remaining butter in the skillet and add the onion and crushed garlic, then cook over medium heat, stirring frequently, for 3–4 minutes, or until soft. Add the wine and stir well, then let the mixture bubble for 2–3 minutes, or until reduced and thickened. Return the mushrooms to the skillet and heat through. The sauce should be thick enough to glaze the mushrooms. Season to taste with salt and pepper.

4 Pile the mushrooms on top of the warm bruschetta, then sprinkle with parsley and serve immediately.

VARIATION
For a slightly different flavor, add chopped tomatoes to the bruschetta. Then grate some cheese on top of the warm mushrooms and tomatoes.

2

Light Bites

warm goat cheese salad

SERVES 4

1 small iceberg lettuce, torn into pieces

handful of arugula leaves

few radicchio leaves, torn

6 slices French bread

4 oz/115 g goat cheese, sliced

dressing

4 tbsp extra virgin olive oil

1 tbsp white wine vinegar

salt and pepper

1 Preheat the broiler. Divide the lettuce, arugula, and radicchio among 4 individual salad bowls.

2 Toast one side of the bread under the broiler until golden. Place a slice of cheese on top of each untoasted side and toast until the cheese is just melting.

3 Place the dressing ingredients in a jar with a screw-top lid. Shake well and pour over the leaves, tossing to coat.

4 Cut each slice of bread in half and place 3 halves on top of each salad. Toss very gently to combine and serve warm.

tomato & feta salad

SERVES 4

2 lb 4 oz/1 kg ripe tomatoes, thickly sliced

8 oz/225 g feta cheese

½ cup extra virgin olive oil

16 black olives, pitted

pepper

1 Arrange the tomato slices in concentric rings on a serving dish. Crumble the feta over the tomatoes and drizzle with the olive oil. Top with the olives.

2 Season to taste with pepper. Salt is probably not necessary because feta is already salty. Let stand for 30 minutes before serving.

moroccan tomato & red bell pepper salad

SERVES 4

3 red bell peppers

4 ripe tomatoes

½ **bunch of fresh cilantro, chopped**

2 garlic cloves, finely chopped

salt and pepper

1 Preheat the broiler. Place the bell peppers on a baking sheet and cook under the broiler, turning occasionally, for 15 minutes. Add the tomatoes and broil, turning occasionally, for an additional 5–10 minutes, or until all the skins are charred and blistered. Remove from the heat and let cool.

2 Peel and seed the bell peppers and tomatoes and slice the flesh thinly. Place in a bowl, mix well, and season with salt and pepper. Sprinkle with the cilantro and garlic, cover with plastic wrap, and chill in the refrigerator for at least 1 hour. Just before serving, drain off any excess liquid.

crunchy thai-style salad

SERVES 4

1 slightly underripe mango

5 romaine lettuce leaves, torn into pieces

1¾ cups bean sprouts

handful of fresh cilantro leaves

¼ cup roasted unsalted peanuts, crushed

dressing

juice of 1 lime

2 tbsp light soy sauce

1 tsp light brown sugar

1 shallot, very thinly sliced

1 garlic clove, finely chopped

1 red Thai chile, very thinly sliced

1 tbsp chopped fresh mint

1 To make the dressing, place all of the dressing ingredients in a bowl. Mix well and set aside.

2 Peel the mango using a sharp knife or vegetable peeler. Slice the flesh from either side and around the pit. Thinly slice or shred the flesh.

3 Put the torn lettuce, bean sprouts, cilantro leaves, and mango in a serving bowl. Gently toss together. Spoon the dressing over the top, sprinkle with the peanuts, and serve immediately.

Step 1

Step 2

Step 3

red onion, tomato & herb salad

SERVES 4

2 lb/900 g tomatoes, sliced thinly

1 tbsp sugar (optional)

1 red onion, sliced thinly

large handful of coarsely chopped, fresh herbs in season, such as tarragon, sorrel, cilantro, or basil

salt and pepper

dressing

2–4 tbsp vegetable oil

2 tbsp red wine vinegar or fruit vinegar

1 Arrange the tomato slices in a shallow bowl. Sprinkle with the sugar, if using, and salt and pepper.

2 Separate the onion slices into rings and sprinkle them over the tomatoes. Sprinkle the herbs over the top.

3 Place all of the dressing ingredients in a jar with a screw-top lid. Shake well. Pour the dressing over the salad and mix gently.

4 Cover with plastic wrap and chill for 20 minutes. Remove the salad from the refrigerator 5 minutes before serving, unwrap the dish, and stir gently before setting out on the table.

wilted spinach, yogurt & walnut salad

SERVES 2

1 lb/450 g fresh spinach leaves

1 onion, chopped

1 tbsp olive oil

1 cup plain yogurt

1 garlic clove, finely chopped

2 tbsp chopped toasted walnuts

2–3 tsp chopped fresh mint

salt and pepper

pita bread, to serve

1 Put the spinach and onion into a pan, cover, and cook gently for a few minutes until the spinach has wilted.

2 Add the oil and cook for an additional 5 minutes. Season with salt and pepper to taste.

3 Combine the yogurt and garlic in a bowl. Put the spinach and onion into a serving bowl and pour over the yogurt mixture. Scatter over the walnuts and chopped mint and serve with pita bread.

green bean & walnut salad

SERVES 2

1 lb/450 g green beans, trimmed

1 small onion, finely chopped

1 garlic clove, chopped

4 tbsp freshly grated Parmesan-style vegetarian cheese

2 tbsp chopped walnuts or almonds, to garnish

dressing

3 tbsp extra virgin olive oil

2 tbsp white wine vinegar

2 tsp chopped fresh tarragon

salt and pepper

1 Cook the green beans in salted boiling water for 3–4 minutes. Drain well, refresh under cold running water, and drain again. Put into a mixing bowl and add the onion, garlic, and cheese.

2 Place all of the dressing ingredients in a jar with a screw-top lid. Shake well. Pour the dressing over the salad and toss gently to coat. Cover with plastic wrap and chill for at least 30 minutes.

3 Remove the beans from the refrigerator 10 minutes before serving. Give them a quick stir and transfer to a shallow serving dish.

4 Toast the nuts in a dry skillet over medium heat for 2 minutes, or until they begin to brown. Sprinkle the toasted nuts over the beans to garnish before serving.

avocado salad with lime dressing

SERVES 4

2¼ oz/60 g mixed red and green lettuce leaves

2¼ oz/60 g wild arugula

4 scallions, finely diced

5 tomatoes, sliced

¼ cup toasted and chopped walnuts

2 avocados

1 tbsp lemon juice

lime dressing

1 tbsp lime juice

1 tsp French mustard

1 tbsp sour cream

1 tbsp chopped fresh parsley or cilantro

3 tbsp extra virgin olive oil

pinch of sugar

salt and pepper

1 Wash and drain the lettuce and arugula, if necessary. Shred all the leaves and arrange in the bottom of a large salad bowl. Add the scallions, tomatoes, and walnuts.

2 Pit, peel, and thinly slice or dice the avocados. Brush with the lemon juice to prevent discoloration, then transfer to the salad bowl. Gently mix together.

3 To make the dressing, put all of the dressing ingredients into a screw-top jar and shake well. Drizzle over the salad and serve immediately.

Step 1

Step 2

Step 3

nutty beet salad

SERVES 4

3 tbsp red wine vinegar or fruit vinegar

3 cooked beets, grated

2 sharp apples

2 tbsp lemon juice

¼ cup chopped pecans

4 large handfuls of mixed salad greens, to serve

dressing

¼ cup plain yogurt

¼ cup mayonnaise

1 garlic clove, chopped

1 tbsp chopped fresh dill

salt and pepper

1 Sprinkle vinegar over the beets, cover with plastic wrap, and chill for at least 4 hours.

2 Core and slice the apples, place the slices in a dish, and sprinkle with the lemon juice.

3 Place all of the dressing ingredients in a jar with a screw-top lid and shake well. Remove the beets from the refrigerator and dress. Add the apples to the beets and mix gently to coat with the salad dressing.

4 Toast the pecans in a heavy, dry skillet over medium heat for 2 minutes, or until they begin to brown.

5 To serve, arrange a handful of salad greens on each plate, top with a large spoonful of the apple-and-beet mixture, and garnish with the toasted pecans.

goat cheese tarts

MAKES 12

butter, for greasing

14 oz/400 g prepared puff pastry

1 tbsp all-purpose flour, for dusting

1 egg, beaten

3 tbsp onion relish or tomato relish

3 goat cheese logs (about 4 oz/115 g each), sliced

extra virgin olive oil, for drizzling

pepper

1 Preheat the oven to 400°F/200°C and grease several baking sheets.

2 Cut out as many 3-inch/7.5-cm circles as possible from the pastry on a lightly floured surface.

3 Place the circles on the baking sheets and press gently, about 1 inch/2.5 cm from the edge of each, with a smaller 2-inch/5-cm round cookie cutter.

4 Brush the circles with beaten egg and prick with a fork. Top each circle with a little relish and a slice of goat cheese. Drizzle with oil and sprinkle over a little pepper.

5 Bake for 8–10 minutes, or until the pastry is crisp and the cheese is bubbling. Serve warm.

nachos with chiles & olives

SERVES 4

2 lb 4 oz/1 kg tortilla chips

6 tbsp chopped pickled jalapeño chiles

⅔ cup pitted and sliced black olives

4 cups grated cheddar cheese

dipping sauce, to serve

1 Preheat the oven to 350°F/180°C. Spread out the tortilla chips in a large ovenproof dish.

2 Sprinkle the chiles, olives, and grated cheese evenly over the tortilla chips and bake for 12–15 minutes, or until the cheese is melted and bubbling. Serve immediately with a dipping sauce of your choice.

quinoa with roasted vegetables

SERVES 2–4

2 bell peppers (any color), seeded and cut into chunky pieces

1 large zucchini, cut into chunks

1 small fennel bulb, cut into slim wedges

1 tbsp olive oil

2 tsp very finely chopped fresh rosemary leaves

1 tsp chopped fresh thyme leaves

generous ½ cup quinoa

1½ cups vegetable stock

2 garlic cloves, peeled and crushed

3 tbsp chopped fresh flat-leaf parsley

⅓ cup pine nuts, toasted

salt and pepper

1 Preheat the oven to 400°F/200°C. Put the bell peppers, zucchini, and fennel in a roasting pan large enough to hold the vegetables in a single layer.

2 Drizzle the olive oil over the vegetables and sprinkle with the rosemary and thyme. Season well with salt and pepper, then mix well with clean hands. Roast for 25–30 minutes, until tender and lightly charred.

3 Meanwhile, put the quinoa, stock, and garlic in a pan. Bring to a boil, cover, and simmer for 12–15 minutes, until tender and most of the stock has been absorbed.

4 Remove the vegetables from the oven. Turn the quinoa into the roasting pan. Add the parsley and pine nuts, and toss together. Serve warm or cold.

Step 1

Step 2

Step 3

broiled provolone with herbed couscous

SERVES 4

1 lb/450 g provolone cheese, cut into ¼-inch/5-mm slices

4 tbsp chili oil

herbed couscous

1¾ cups hot vegetable stock

heaping 1 cup couscous

2 tbsp chopped fresh mixed herbs

2 tsp lemon juice

1 tbsp olive oil

1 Preheat the broiler to high and line the broiler rack with foil.

2 Put the cheese slices in a bowl, pour over the chili oil, and toss well to coat the cheese.

3 Place the cheese on the broiler rack and cook under the broiler for 2–3 minutes on each side, until golden.

4 Meanwhile, stir the hot stock into the couscous in a large bowl. Cover and let stand for 5 minutes.

5 Stir the herbs, lemon juice, and olive oil into the couscous and serve with the broiled provolone cheese.

baked chile cheese sandwiches

MAKES 4

3½ cups grated cheese, such as cheddar

½ cup butter, softened, plus extra for baking

4 fresh green chiles, seeded and chopped

½ tsp ground cumin

8 thick slices bread

1 Preheat the oven to 375°F/190°C. Mix together the cheese and butter in a bowl until creamy, then add the chiles and cumin.

2 Spread this mixture over 4 slices of bread and top with the remaining slices.

3 Spread the outside of the sandwiches with extra butter and bake for 8–10 minutes, until crisp. Serve.

cheese baked zucchini

SERVES 4

4 medium zucchini

2 tbsp extra virgin olive oil

4 oz/115 g mozzarella cheese, thinly sliced

2 large tomatoes, seeded and diced

2 tsp chopped fresh basil or oregano

1 Preheat the oven to 400°F/200°C. Slice the zucchini lengthwise into 4 strips each. Brush with the oil and place on a baking sheet.

2 Bake the zucchini in the oven for 10 minutes, without letting them get too floppy.

3 Remove the zucchini from the oven. Arrange the slices of cheese on top and sprinkle with diced tomato and basil. Return to the oven for 5 minutes, or until the cheese has melted.

4 Remove the zucchini from the oven and transfer carefully to serving plates.

thai tofu cakes with chile dip

SERVES 8

1¼ cups coarsely grated firm tofu

1 lemongrass stalk, outer layer discarded, finely chopped

2 garlic cloves, chopped

1-inch/2.5-cm piece fresh ginger, grated

2 kaffir lime leaves, finely chopped (optional)

2 shallots, finely chopped

2 fresh red chiles, seeded and finely chopped

4 tbsp chopped fresh cilantro

scant ¾ cup all-purpose flour, plus extra for flouring

½ tsp salt

corn oil, for cooking

chile dip

3 tbsp white distilled vinegar or rice wine vinegar

2 scallions, finely sliced

1 tbsp superfine sugar

2 fresh chiles, finely chopped

2 tbsp chopped fresh cilantro

pinch of salt

1 To make the chile dip, mix all of the ingredients together in a small serving bowl and set aside.

2 Mix the tofu with the lemongrass, garlic, ginger, lime leaves, if using, shallots, chiles, and cilantro in a mixing bowl. Stir in the flour and salt to make a coarse, sticky paste. Cover and let chill in the refrigerator for 1 hour to let the mixture firm up slightly.

3 Form the mixture into 8 large walnut-size balls and, using floured hands, flatten into circles. Heat enough oil to cover the bottom of a large, heavy-bottom skillet over medium heat. Cook the cakes in 2 batches, turning halfway through, for 4–6 minutes, or until golden brown. Drain on paper towels and serve warm with the chile dip.

Step 1

Step 2

Step 3

potato, leek & feta patties

SERVES 4

1 whole garlic bulb

heaping 1 cup peeled sweet potato chunks

1¼ cups peeled and chopped carrots

1⅓ cups trimmed and finely chopped leeks

⅓ cup crumbled feta cheese

1–2 tsp Tabasco sauce, or to taste

1 tbsp chopped fresh cilantro

pepper

fresh herbs or salad, to garnish

ketchup, to serve (optional)

1 Preheat the oven to 375°F/190°C. Break the garlic bulb open, place in a small roasting pan, and roast for 20 minutes, or until soft. Remove and when cool enough to handle, squeeze out the roasted garlic flesh.

2 Cook the sweet potato and carrots in a large pan of boiling water for 15 minutes, or until soft. Drain and mash, then mix in the roasted garlic flesh.

3 Add the leeks, feta cheese, Tabasco sauce, cilantro, and pepper to taste to the potato mixture. Cover and let chill in the refrigerator for at least 30 minutes.

4 Using slightly dampened hands, shape the sweet potato mixture into 8 small round patties and place on a nonstick baking sheet. Bake for 15–20 minutes, or until piping hot. Garnish with fresh herbs and serve with ketchup, if using.

tomato ratatouille

SERVES 4

4 sprays olive oil

1 onion, cut into small wedges

2–4 garlic cloves, chopped

1 small eggplant, trimmed and chopped

1 small red bell pepper, seeded and chopped

1 small yellow bell pepper, seeded and chopped

1 zucchini, trimmed and chopped

2 tbsp tomato paste

3 tbsp water

4 oz/115 g mushrooms, sliced if large

1¼ cups chopped ripe tomatoes

pepper

1 tbsp shredded fresh basil, to garnish

1 oz/25 g Parmesan-style vegetarian cheese, freshly shaved, to serve

1 Heat a heavy-bottom pan and spray with the oil. Add the onion, garlic, and eggplant and cook, stirring frequently, for 3 minutes.

2 Add the bell peppers and zucchini. Mix the tomato paste and water together in a small bowl and stir into the pan. Bring to a boil, cover with a lid, reduce the heat to a simmer, and cook for 10 minutes.

3 Add the mushrooms and chopped tomatoes with pepper to taste and continue to simmer for 12–15 minutes, stirring occasionally, until the vegetables are tender.

4 Divide the ratatouille among 4 warm bowls, garnish each with shredded basil, and serve with freshly shaved Parmesan-style vegetarian cheese to sprinkle over.

spicy stuffed bell peppers

SERVES 4

4 assorted colored bell peppers

3 sprays olive oil

1 onion, finely chopped

2 garlic cloves, chopped

1-inch/2.5-cm piece fresh ginger, peeled and grated

1–2 fresh serrano chiles, seeded and chopped

1 tsp ground cumin

1 tsp ground coriander

scant ½ cup cooked brown basmati rice

1 cup peeled and grated carrots

¾ cup trimmed and grated zucchini

scant ¼ cup finely chopped plumped dried apricots

1 tbsp chopped fresh cilantro

⅔ cup water

pepper

fresh herbs, to garnish

1 Preheat the oven to 375°F/190°C. Cut the tops off the bell peppers and set aside for "lids". Discard the seeds from each pepper. Place the peppers in a large bowl and cover with boiling water. Let soak for 10 minutes, then drain and set aside.

2 Heat a nonstick skillet and spray with the oil. Add the onion, garlic, ginger, and chiles and sauté for 3 minutes, stirring frequently. Sprinkle in the ground spices and continue to cook for an additional 2 minutes.

3 Remove the skillet from the heat and stir in the rice, carrot, zucchini, apricots, chopped cilantro, and pepper to taste. Stir well, then use to stuff the peppers.

4 Place the stuffed peppers in an ovenproof dish large enough to let the peppers stand upright. Put the reserved tops in position. Pour the water around their bottoms, cover loosely with the "lids" or foil, and cook for 25–30 minutes, or until piping hot. Serve garnished with herbs.

stir-fried rice with green vegetables

SERVES 4

1¼ cups jasmine rice

2 tbsp vegetable or peanut oil

1 tbsp green curry paste

6 scallions, sliced

2 garlic cloves, crushed

1 zucchini, cut into thin sticks

4 oz/115 g green beans

6 oz/175 g asparagus spears, trimmed

3–4 fresh Thai basil leaves

1 Cook the rice in lightly salted boiling water for 12–15 minutes, drain well, then cool thoroughly and chill overnight.

2 Heat the oil in a wok and stir-fry the curry paste for 1 minute. Add the scallions and garlic and stir-fry for 1 minute.

3 Add the zucchini, beans, and asparagus, and stir-fry for 3–4 minutes, until just tender. Break up the rice and add it to the wok. Cook, stirring continuously, for 2–3 minutes, until the rice is hot. Stir in the basil leaves and serve immediately.

Step 1

Step 2

Step 3

spicy chickpea burgers

SERVES 4

1 lb 12 oz/800 g canned chickpeas, drained and rinsed

1 small onion, chopped

zest and juice of 1 lime

2 tsp ground coriander

2 tsp ground cumin

6 tbsp all-purpose flour

4 tbsp olive oil

4 fresh basil sprigs, to garnish

tomato salsa, to serve

1 Put the chickpeas, onion, lime zest and juice, and the spices into a food processor and process to a coarse paste.

2 Turn the mixture out onto a clean surface or cutting board and shape into 4 patties.

3 Spread the flour out on a large flat plate and use to coat the patties.

4 Heat the oil in a large skillet, add the burgers, and cook for 2 minutes on each side, until crisp. Garnish with basil and serve with tomato salsa.

open potato omelet

SERVES 4

⅓ **cup peeled and grated old potato**

1 onion, grated

2 garlic cloves, crushed

1 cup peeled and grated carrot

4 sprays olive oil

1 yellow bell pepper, peeled and thinly sliced

¾ **cup trimmed and thinly sliced zucchini**

6 cherry tomatoes, halved

2 eggs

3 egg whites

1 tbsp snipped fresh chives

pepper

fresh arugula, to garnish

1 Put the grated potato into a large bowl and cover with cold water. Let stand for 15 minutes, then drain, rinse thoroughly, and dry on absorbent paper towels or a clean dish towel. Mix with the grated onion, garlic, and carrot.

2 Heat a heavy-bottom nonstick skillet and spray with the oil. Add the potato-and-carrot mixture and cook over low heat for 5 minutes, pressing the vegetables down firmly with a spatula. Add the peeled bell pepper and zucchini slices. Cover with a lid or crumpled piece of foil and cook very gently, stirring occasionally, for 5 minutes.

3 Add the halved cherry tomatoes and cook for an additional 2 minutes, or until the vegetables are tender.

4 Beat the whole eggs, egg whites, pepper to taste, and chives together in a bowl. Pour over the vegetable mixture and cook for 4–5 minutes, stirring the egg from the sides of the skillet toward the center, until the vegetables are tender and the eggs are set. Serve immediately, garnished with arugula leaves.

zucchini, carrot & tomato frittata

SERVES 4

2 sprays olive oil

1 onion, cut into small wedges

1–2 garlic cloves, crushed

2 eggs

2 egg whites

¾ cup trimmed and grated zucchini

1 cup peeled and grated carrots

2 tomatoes, chopped

pepper

1 tbsp shredded fresh basil, for sprinkling

1 Heat a large nonstick skillet and spray with the oil. Add the onion and garlic, and sauté for 5 minutes, stirring frequently. Beat the eggs and egg whites together in a bowl, then pour into the skillet. Using a spatula or fork, pull the egg mixture from the sides of the skillet into the center, letting the uncooked egg take its place.

2 Once the bottom has set lightly, add the grated zucchini and carrots with the tomatoes. Add pepper to taste and continue to cook over low heat until the eggs are set to personal preference.

3 Sprinkle with the shredded basil, cut the frittata into quarters, and serve.

leek & goat cheese crepes

MAKES 8

2 tbsp unsalted butter

½ tbsp sunflower oil

2¼ cups halved, rinsed, and shredded leeks

freshly grated nutmeg, to taste

1 tbsp finely snipped fresh chives

8 savory crepes

3 oz/85 g soft goat cheese, rind removed if necessary, chopped

salt and pepper

1 Preheat the oven to 400°F/200°C. Melt the butter with the oil in a heavy-bottom saucepan with a lid over medium–high heat. Add the leeks and stir around so that they are well coated. Stir in salt and pepper to taste, but remember the cheese might be salty. Add a few gratings of nutmeg, then cover the leeks with a sheet of wet wax paper and put the lid on the saucepan. Reduce the heat to very low and let the leeks sweat for 5–7 minutes, until very tender but not brown. Stir in the chives, then taste and adjust the seasoning, if necessary.

2 Put 1 crepe on a work surface and put one-eighth of the leeks on the crepe. Top with one-eighth of the cheese, then fold the crepe into a square pocket or simply roll it around the filling. Place the stuffed crepe on a baking sheet, then continue to fill and fold, or roll, the remaining crepes.

3 Put the baking sheet in the oven and bake for 5 minutes, or until the crepes are hot and the cheese starts to melt. Serve hot.

VARIATION
Replace the goat cheese with your favorite cheese to add a different flavor. For a stronger cheese taste, sprinkle some grated cheese or small chunks over the top of the crepes before baking.

3

Marvelous Mains

tofu stir-fry

SERVES 4

2 tbsp sunflower or olive oil

12 oz/350 g firm tofu, cubed

2½ cups coarsely chopped bok choy

1 garlic clove, chopped

4 tbsp sweet chili sauce

2 tbsp light soy sauce

1 Heat 1 tablespoon of the oil in a wok, add the tofu in batches, and stir-fry for 2–3 minutes, until golden. Remove and set aside.

2 Add the bok choy to the wok and stir-fry for a few seconds until tender and wilted. Remove and set aside.

3 Add the remaining oil to the wok, then add the garlic and stir-fry for 30 seconds.

4 Stir in the chili sauce and soy sauce and bring to a boil. Return the tofu and bok choy to the wok and toss gently until coated in the sauce. Serve immediately.

summer stir-fry

SERVES 4

2 tbsp peanut or corn oil

1 tsp finely chopped fresh ginger

2 garlic cloves, finely chopped

1 cup sliced green beans

1 cup sliced sugar snap peas

1⅔ cups broccoli florets

1 cup sliced carrots

4 oz/115 g asparagus spears, sliced

½ red bell pepper, seeded and sliced

½ orange bell pepper, seeded and sliced

½ yellow bell pepper, seeded and sliced

2 celery stalks, sliced

3 scallions, trimmed and sliced

salt

1 Heat half of the oil in a preheated wok or heavy-bottom skillet. Add the ginger and garlic and stir-fry for a few seconds, then add the green beans and stir-fry for 2 minutes.

2 Add the sugar snap peas, stir-fry for 1 minute, then add the broccoli florets, carrots, and asparagus and stir-fry for 2 minutes.

3 Add the remaining oil, the bell peppers, celery, and scallions and stir-fry for an additional 2–3 minutes, or until all the vegetables are crisp and tender. Season to taste with salt and serve immediately.

noodle stir-fry

SERVES 2

5 oz/140 g flat rice noodles

6 tbsp soy sauce

2 tbsp lemon juice

1 tsp granulated sugar

½ tsp cornstarch

1 tbsp vegetable oil

2 tsp grated fresh ginger

2 garlic cloves, chopped

4–5 scallions, trimmed and sliced

2 tbsp rice wine or dry sherry

7 oz/200 g canned water chestnuts, sliced

1 Put the noodles in a large bowl, cover with boiling water, and let stand for 4 minutes, or according to the package instructions. Drain and rinse under cold running water.

2 Mix the soy sauce, lemon juice, sugar, and cornstarch together in a small bowl.

3 Heat the oil in a wok, add the ginger and garlic, and stir-fry for 1 minute. Add the scallions and stir-fry for 3 minutes.

4 Add the rice wine followed by the soy sauce mixture and cook for 1 minute.

5 Stir in the water chestnuts and noodles and cook for an additional 1–2 minutes, or until heated through. Serve immediately.

bean burgers

SERVES 4

**1 tbsp sunflower oil,
plus extra for brushing**

1 onion, finely chopped

**1 garlic clove,
finely chopped**

1 tsp ground coriander

1 tsp ground cumin

**1 ⅔ cups finely chopped
white mushrooms**

**15 oz/425 g canned pinto
or red kidney beans,
drained and rinsed**

**2 tbsp chopped fresh
flat-leaf parsley**

**all-purpose flour,
for dusting**

salt and pepper

**hamburger buns
and salad, to serve**

1 Heat the oil in a heavy-bottom skillet over medium heat. Add the onion and cook, stirring frequently, for 5 minutes, or until softened. Add the garlic, coriander, and cumin and cook, stirring, for an additional minute. Add the mushrooms and cook, stirring frequently, for 4–5 minutes, until all the liquid has evaporated. Transfer to a bowl.

2 Put the beans in a small bowl and mash with a fork. Stir into the mushroom mixture with the parsley and season with salt and pepper.

3 Preheat the broiler to medium–high. Divide the mixture equally into 4 portions, dust lightly with flour, and shape into flat, round patties. Brush with oil and cook under the broiler for 4–5 minutes on each side. Serve in hamburger buns with salad.

Step 1

Step 2

Step 3

vegetable chili

SERVES 4

**1 eggplant, cut into
1-inch/2.5-cm slices**

**1 tbsp olive oil, plus extra
for brushing**

**1 large red onion,
finely chopped**

**2 red or yellow bell
peppers, seeded and
finely chopped**

**3–4 garlic cloves, finely
chopped or crushed**

**1 lb 12 oz/800 g canned
chopped tomatoes**

1 tbsp mild chili powder

½ tsp ground cumin

½ tsp dried oregano

**2 small zucchini, cut into
quarters, lengthwise,
and sliced**

**14 oz/400 g canned kidney
beans, drained and
rinsed**

2 cups water

1 tbsp tomato paste

salt and pepper

**6 scallions, finely chopped
and generous 1 cup
grated cheese, to garnish**

1 Brush the eggplant slices on one side with olive oil. Heat half of the oil in a large, heavy-bottom skillet over medium–high heat. Add the eggplant slices, oiled-side up, and cook for 5–6 minutes, or until browned on one side. Turn the slices over, cook on the other side until browned, and transfer to a plate. Cut into bite-size pieces.

2 Heat the remaining oil in a large pan over medium heat. Add the onion and bell peppers and cook, stirring occasionally, for 3–4 minutes, or until the onion is softened, but not browned.

3 Add the garlic and cook for an additional 2–3 minutes, or until the onion is beginning to color.

4 Add the tomatoes, chili powder, cumin, and oregano. Season to taste with salt and pepper. Bring just to a boil, reduce the heat, cover, and simmer gently for 15 minutes.

5 Add the zucchini, eggplant pieces, and kidney beans. Stir in the water and tomato paste. Return to a boil, then cover and continue simmering for 45 minutes, or until the vegetables are tender. Taste and adjust the seasoning, if necessary. Ladle into warm serving bowls and garnish with scallions and cheese.

leek & spinach tart

SERVES 6–8

8 oz/225 g prepared puff pastry

2 tbsp unsalted butter

2 leeks, sliced finely

4 cups chopped fresh spinach

2 eggs

1¼ cups heavy cream

pinch of dried thyme

salt and pepper

1 Roll the pastry into a rectangle about 10 x 12 inches/ 25 x 30 cm. Let rest for 5 minutes, then press into a 8 x 10 inch/20 x 25 cm quiche pan. Do not trim the overhang. Cover the pastry with foil and chill in the refrigerator. Preheat the oven to 350°F/180°C.

2 Melt the butter in a large skillet over medium heat. Add the leeks, stir, and cook gently for 5 minutes, or until soft. Add the spinach and cook for 3 minutes, or until soft. Let cool.

3 Beat the eggs in a bowl. Stir in the cream and season with thyme and salt and pepper. Remove the pie shell from the refrigerator and uncover. Spread the cooked vegetables over the bottom. Pour in the egg mixture.

4 Place on a baking sheet and bake for 30 minutes, or until set. Remove the tart from the oven and let rest for 10 minutes before serving. Serve directly from the quiche pan.

cheese & vegetable tart

12 oz/350 g prepared, unsweetened pie dough, thawed if frozen

10 oz/280 g mixed frozen vegetables

⅔ cup heavy cream

1 cup grated cheddar cheese

salt and pepper

basil leaves, to garnish

1 Thinly roll out the dough on a lightly floured surface and use to line a 9-inch/23-cm tart pan. Prick the bottom and chill in the refrigerator for 30 minutes. Preheat the oven to 400°F/200°C.

2 Line the pastry shell with foil and fill halfway with dried beans. Place the pan on a baking sheet and bake for 15–20 minutes, or until just firm. Remove the beans and foil, return the pastry shell to the oven, and bake for an additional 5–7 minutes, until golden. Remove the pastry shell from the oven and let cool in the pan.

3 Meanwhile, cook the frozen vegetables in a pan of salted boiling water. Drain and let cool.

4 When ready to cook, preheat the oven again to 400°F/200°C. Mix the cooked vegetables and cream together and season with salt and pepper. Spoon the mixture evenly into the pastry shell and sprinkle with the cheese. Bake for 15 minutes, or until the cheese has melted and is turning golden. Serve hot or cold, garnished with basil leaves.

mushroom & onion quiche

SERVES 4

butter, for greasing

1 quantity pie dough, chilled

all-purpose flour, for dusting

filling

4 tbsp unsalted butter

3 red onions, halved and sliced

12 oz/350 g mixed wild mushrooms, such as porcini, chanterelles, and morels

2 tsp chopped fresh thyme

1 egg

2 egg yolks

generous ⅓ cup heavy cream

salt and pepper

1 Preheat the oven to 375°F/190°C. Lightly grease a 9-inch/23-cm loose-bottom quiche pan. Roll out the dough on a lightly floured surface and use to line the pan. Line the pastry shell with parchment paper and fill with dried beans. Chill in the refrigerator for 30 minutes. Bake in the preheated oven for 25 minutes. Remove the paper and beans and cool on a wire rack. Reduce the oven temperature to 350°F/180°C.

2 To make the filling, melt the butter in a large, heavy-bottom skillet over very low heat. Add the onions, cover, and cook, stirring occasionally, for 20 minutes. Add the mushrooms and thyme and cook, stirring occasionally, for an additional 10 minutes. Spoon into the pastry shell and put the pan on a baking sheet.

3 Lightly beat the egg, egg yolks, cream, and salt and pepper to taste in a bowl. Pour over the mushroom mixture. Bake in the oven for 20 minutes, or until the filling is set and golden. Serve hot or at room temperature.

Step 1

Step 2

Step 3

caramelized onion tart

7 tbsp unsalted butter

4 onions (about 1 lb 5 oz/600 g), thinly sliced

2 eggs

scant ½ cup heavy cream

scant 1 cup grated Swiss cheese

8-inch/20-cm baked pie shell

generous 1 cup grated Parmesan-style vegetarian cheese

salt and pepper

1 Melt the butter over medium heat in a heavy skillet. Stir in the onions and cook until they are well browned and caramelized. (This will take up to 30 minutes, depending on the width of the skillet.) Stir frequently to avoid burning. Remove the onions from the skillet and set aside. Preheat the oven to 375°F/190°C.

2 Beat the eggs in a large mixing bowl, stir in the cream, and season with salt and pepper. Add the Swiss cheese and mix well. Mix in the cooked onions.

3 Pour the egg-and-onion mixture into the baked pie shell, sprinkle with Parmesan-style vegetarian cheese, and place on a baking sheet. Bake for 15–20 minutes, or until the filling has set and begun to brown.

4 Remove from the oven and let rest for at least 10 minutes. The tart can be served hot or let cool to room temperature.

potato & cabbage casserole

SERVES 4

**3 cups peeled and diced
mealy potatoes**

2 tbsp milk

**4 tbsp butter, plus extra
for greasing**

**2½ cups shredded green
cabbage**

**1½ cups thinly sliced
carrots**

1 medium onion, chopped

**½ cup grated cheddar
cheese**

salt and pepper

1 Cook the potatoes in salted water for 10 minutes, or until softened. Drain well and turn into a large mixing bowl. Mash until smooth. Beat with the milk, half of the butter, and salt and pepper to taste.

2 Cook the cabbage and carrots separately in salted boiling water for 5 minutes. Drain well. Combine the cabbage with the potatoes. Melt the remaining butter in a small skillet and cook the onion over medium heat until softened but not browned. Preheat the oven to 375°F/190°C. Grease a shallow ovenproof dish.

3 Spread a layer of mashed potatoes in the bottom of the prepared ovenproof dish. Layer the onions on top, then the carrots. Repeat to use up all of the ingredients, finishing with a layer of potato.

4 Sprinkle the grated cheese on top, place the dish in the oven, and bake for 45 minutes, or until the top is golden and crusty. Remove from the oven and serve immediately.

leek & egg casserole

SERVES 4

6 tbsp butter

4 leeks, trimmed and sliced

8 hard-cooked eggs, shelled and quartered

sauce

scant ½ cup all-purpose flour

1¼ cups milk

½ cup grated cheddar or Emmental cheese

1 tsp whole-grain mustard

cayenne pepper (optional)

salt and pepper

1 Melt 2 tablespoons of the butter in a skillet over medium heat, add the leeks, and cook. Remove when soft and add to an ovenproof dish. Arrange the egg quarters on top and season to taste. Preheat the broiler to high.

2 For the sauce, melt the remaining butter in a small pan over medium heat. Gradually add the flour, stirring continuously, until it has been absorbed. Still stirring, slowly add the milk until blended. Bring the sauce to a boil, reduce the heat, and simmer, stirring, until it thickens. Add the cheese, mustard, and cayenne pepper, if using, stirring until well blended.

3 Pour the sauce over the eggs and leeks. Put the dish under the broiler for 2–3 minutes. Serve when bubbling.

butternut squash & mushroom risotto

SERVES 4

2 tbsp olive oil

1 large onion, finely chopped

6 sage leaves, finely chopped

2 tsp chopped fresh thyme leaves

5⅓ cups ¾-inch/2-cm butternut squash chunks

3¼ cups sliced cremini mushrooms

1¼ cups vegetable stock

scant 1 cup dry white wine

1¾ cups risotto rice

⅔ cup grated Parmesan-style vegetarian cheese

salt and pepper

crispy fried sage leaves, to garnish

1 Preheat the oven to 400°F/200°C. Heat the oil in a flameproof casserole on the stove. Add the onion, sage, and thyme. Cover and cook over low heat for 5 minutes, until the onion turns translucent.

2 Stir in the butternut squash, mushrooms, stock, and wine. Bring to a boil, then remove from the heat and stir in the rice.

3 Cover the casserole with a tight-fitting lid and bake in the preheated oven for 40–45 minutes, until the rice and vegetables are tender. Stir in half of the cheese, then season with salt and pepper. Serve immediately, sprinkled with the remaining cheese and fried sage leaves to garnish.

Step 1

Step 2

Step 2

mushroom & cauliflower cheese crumble

SERVES 4

1 medium cauliflower

4 tbsp butter

1⅔ cups sliced white mushrooms

salt and pepper

topping

1⅔ cups dry breadcrumbs

2 tbsp grated Parmesan-style vegetarian cheese

1 tsp dried oregano

1 tsp dried parsley

4 tbsp butter

1 Preheat the oven to 450°F/230°C. Bring a large pan of salted water to a boil. Break the cauliflower into small florets and cook in the boiling water for 3 minutes. Remove from the heat, drain well, and transfer to a large, shallow ovenproof dish.

2 Melt the butter in a small skillet over medium heat. Add the sliced mushrooms, stir to coat, and cook gently for 3 minutes. Remove from the heat and add to the cauliflower. Season with salt and pepper.

3 For the topping, combine the breadcrumbs, cheese, and herbs in a small mixing bowl, then sprinkle the crumbs over the vegetables.

4 Dice the butter for the topping and dot it over the crumbs. Place the dish in the oven and bake for 15 minutes, or until the crumbs are golden brown and crisp. Serve from the dish.

pizza turnovers

SERVES 4

4 individual prepared pizza crusts, 8 inches/20 cm each

filling

2 tbsp olive oil, plus extra for oiling

1 red onion, thinly sliced

1 garlic clove, finely chopped

14 oz/400 g canned chopped tomatoes

⅓ cup pitted black olives

7 oz/200 g mozzarella cheese, drained and diced

1 tbsp chopped fresh oregano

1 Preheat the oven to 400°F/200°C. Lightly oil 2 baking sheets. Heat the oil in a skillet. Add the onion and garlic and cook for 5 minutes, until softened. Add the tomatoes and cook for an additional 5 minutes. Stir in the olives.

2 Divide the tomato mixture among the pizza crusts, spreading it over half of each almost to the edge. Sprinkle over the mozzarella and oregano. Brush the edges with a little water, then fold in half and press to seal.

3 Transfer the turnovers to the prepared baking sheets and bake in the preheated oven for about 15 minutes, until golden and crispy. Let stand for 2 minutes before serving.

cheese & tomato pizza

SERVES 2

oil, for oiling

1 prepared pizza crust, about 10 inches/25 cm

topping

6 tomatoes, thinly sliced

6 oz/175 g mozzarella cheese, drained and thinly sliced

2 tbsp shredded fresh basil

2 tbsp olive oil

salt and pepper

1 Preheat the oven to 450°F/230°C. Lightly oil a baking sheet. Place the pizza crust on the prepared baking sheet.

2 For the topping, arrange the tomato and mozzarella slices over the pizza crust. Season to taste with salt and pepper, sprinkle with the basil, and drizzle with the oil. Bake in the preheated oven for 20–25 minutes, until golden brown. Cut into slices and serve immediately.

ricotta, spinach & pine nut pizza

SERVES 2–4

**2 tbsp olive oil,
plus extra for brushing
and drizzling**

**1 pizza crust, about
10 inches/25 cm**

12 oz/350 g spinach

1 onion, thinly sliced

6 tbsp ricotta cheese

**½ tsp freshly grated
nutmeg**

2 tbsp pine nuts

**4 oz/115 g fontina cheese,
thinly sliced**

salt and pepper

1 Preheat the oven to 425°F/220°C. Lightly oil a baking sheet. Place the pizza crust on the prepared baking sheet.

2 Wash the spinach in cold water and dry well. Heat the oil in a skillet, add the onion, and cook until soft and translucent. Add the spinach and cook, stirring, until just wilted. Remove the skillet from the heat and drain off any liquid.

3 Spread the ricotta cheese evenly over the pizza crust, then cover with the spinach-and-onion mixture. Sprinkle over the nutmeg and pine nuts and season to taste with salt and pepper. Top with the slices of fontina and drizzle with olive oil. Bake in the oven for 20–30 minutes, until golden and sizzling. Serve immediately.

Step 1

Step 2

Step 3

mozzarella gnocchi

SERVES 2–4

butter, for greasing

1 lb/450 g package potato gnocchi

scant 1 cup heavy cream

2 cups grated or chopped firm mozzarella cheese

salt and pepper

1 Preheat the broiler and grease a large baking dish. Cook the gnocchi in a large pan of boiling salted water for about 3 minutes, or according to the package directions. Drain and put into the prepared baking dish.

2 Season the cream with salt and pepper and drizzle over the gnocchi. Scatter over the cheese and cook under the broiler for a few minutes until the top is browned and bubbling. Serve immediately.

vegetarian lasagne

SERVES 4

¼ **cup butter, plus extra for greasing**

1½ **oz/40 g dried porcini mushrooms**

2 **tbsp olive oil**

1 **onion, finely chopped**

14 **oz/400 g canned chopped tomatoes**

1 **lb/450 g white mushrooms, thinly sliced**

1 **garlic clove, finely chopped**

1 **tbsp lemon juice**

½ **tsp Dijon mustard**

large jar of store-bought cheese sauce

6 **lasagna noodles, cooked according to package directions**

½ **cup freshly grated Parmesan-style vegetarian cheese**

salt and pepper

1 Lightly grease an ovenproof dish with butter. Preheat the oven to 400°F/200°C. Place the porcini mushrooms in a small bowl, cover with boiling water, and let soak for 30 minutes. Meanwhile, heat the oil in a small skillet. Add the chopped onion and cook, stirring occasionally, for 5 minutes, or until softened. Add the tomatoes and cook, stirring frequently, for 7–8 minutes. Season with salt and pepper and reserve.

2 Drain and slice the porcini mushrooms. Melt half of the butter in a large, heavy-bottom skillet. Add the porcini and white mushrooms and cook until they begin to release their juices. Add the garlic and lemon juice and season to taste with salt and pepper. Cook over low heat, stirring occasionally, until almost all the liquid has evaporated.

3 Stir the mustard into the cheese sauce, then spread a layer over the bottom of the prepared dish. Place a layer of lasagna noodles on top, cover with the mushrooms, another layer of sauce, another layer of noodles, the tomato mixture, and finally, another layer of sauce. Sprinkle with the Parmesan-style vegetarian cheese and dot with the remaining butter. Bake in the preheated oven for 20 minutes. Let stand for 5 minutes before serving.

pasta with tomatoes & spinach

SERVES 4

1 lb/450 g dried orecchiette or other pasta shapes

3 tbsp olive oil

8 oz/225 g fresh baby spinach leaves, tough stalks removed

1 lb/450 g cherry tomatoes, halved

Parmesan-style vegetarian cheese, grated (optional)

salt and pepper

1 Cook the pasta in a large pan of boiling salted water for 10–12 minutes, or according to the package directions, until tender but still firm to the bite.

2 Heat the oil in a pan, add the spinach and tomatoes, and cook, gently stirring occasionally, for 2–3 minutes, or until the spinach has wilted and the tomatoes are heated through but not disintegrating.

3 Drain the pasta and add it to the pan of vegetables. Toss gently, season with salt and pepper, sprinkle over some Parmesan-style vegetarian cheese, if using, and serve immediately.

macaroni & cheese

SERVES 4

butter or oil, for greasing

8 oz/225 g dried macaroni

generous 1 cup ricotta cheese

1½ tbsp whole-grain mustard

3 tbsp snipped fresh chives

12 cherry tomatoes, halved

scant 1 cup chopped drained sun-dried tomatoes in oil

scant 1 cup grated cheddar cheese

salt and pepper

1 Preheat the broiler to high. Grease a 7½-cup shallow ovenproof dish. Bring a large saucepan of lightly salted water to a boil. Add the pasta, bring back to a boil, and cook for 2–3 minutes, or according to the package directions, until tender but still firm to the bite. Drain.

2 Mix together the ricotta, mustard, and chives with salt and pepper to taste. Stir in the macaroni, cherry tomatoes, and sun-dried tomatoes. Spoon in the macaroni, spreading evenly

3 Sprinkle the cheddar cheese over the macaroni mixture and cook under the preheated broiler for 4–5 minutes, until golden and bubbling. Serve immediately.

Step
2

Step
2

Step
3

pasta with olive sauce

SERVES 2–4

**12 oz/350 g fresh pasta
shapes**

½ tsp salt

6 tbsp olive oil

**½ tsp freshly grated
nutmeg**

½ tsp black pepper

1 garlic clove, crushed

2 tbsp tapenade

**½ cup pitted and sliced
black or green olives**

**1 tbsp chopped fresh
parsley, to garnish
(optional)**

1 Bring a large saucepan of lightly salted water to a boil. Add the pasta, bring back to a boil, and cook for 2–3 minutes, or according to the package directions, until tender but still firm to the bite.

2 Meanwhile, put the salt with the oil, nutmeg, pepper, garlic, tapenade, and olives in another saucepan and heat slowly, but do not let boil. Cover and let stand for 3–4 minutes.

3 Drain the pasta and return to the pan. Add the olives in the flavored oil and heat gently for 1–2 minutes. Serve immediately, garnished with chopped parsley, if using.

chile broccoli pasta

SERVES 4

8 oz/225 g dry penne or macaroni

1 medium head broccoli

¼ cup extra virgin olive oil

2 large garlic cloves, chopped

2 fresh red chiles, seeded and diced

8 cherry tomatoes (optional)

small handful of fresh basil or parsley, to garnish

salt

1 Bring a large saucepan of lightly salted water to a boil. Add the pasta, bring back to a boil, and cook for 8–10 minutes, or according to the package directions, until tender but still firm to the bite. Remove from the heat, drain, rinse with cold water, and drain again. Set aside.

2 Cut the broccoli into florets and cook in salted boiling water for 5 minutes. Drain, rinse with cold water, drain again, and set aside.

3 Heat the olive oil in the pan that the pasta was cooked in. Add the garlic, chiles, and tomatoes, if using. Cook over high heat for 1 minute.

4 Add the broccoli to the pan with the flavored oil and mix well. Cook for 2 minutes to heat through. Add the pasta and mix well again. Cook for an additional 1 minute.

5 Remove the pasta from the heat, turn into a large serving bowl, and serve garnished with basil or parsley.

creamy ricotta, mint & garlic pasta

SERVES 4

10½ oz/300 g short fresh pasta shapes

heaping ½ cup ricotta cheese

1–2 roasted garlic cloves from a jar, finely chopped

⅔ cup heavy cream

1 tbsp chopped fresh mint, plus 4 sprigs to garnish

salt and pepper

1 Bring a large saucepan of lightly salted water to a boil. Add the pasta, bring back to a boil, and cook for 2–3 minutes, or according to the package directions, until tender but still firm to the bite.

2 Beat the ricotta, garlic, cream, and chopped mint together in a bowl until smooth.

3 Drain the cooked pasta, then turn back into the pan. Pour in the cheese mixture and toss together.

4 Season with pepper and serve immediately, garnished with the sprigs of mint.

spaghetti with parsley & parmesan

SERVES 4

1 lb/450 g dried spaghetti

¾ cup unsalted butter

¼ cup chopped fresh flat-leaf parsley

2¼ cups grated Parmesan-style vegetarian cheese

salt

1 Bring a large saucepan of lightly salted water to a boil. Add the pasta, bring back to a boil, and cook for 8–10 minutes, or according to the package directions, until tender but still firm to the bite. Drain and turn into a warm serving dish.

2 Add the butter, parsley, and half of the cheese and toss well, using 2 forks, until the butter and cheese have melted. Sprinkle with the remaining cheese and serve immediately.

VARIATION

For a bit of color, add a handful of cherry tomatoes to the dish. Cut them in half and add them to the pasta with the butter and parsley.

4

Sensational
Sides

potatoes dauphinois

SERVES 4

1 tbsp butter

3 large waxy potatoes, sliced

2 garlic cloves, crushed

1 red onion, sliced

¾ cup grated Swiss cheese

1¼ cups heavy cream

salt and pepper

1 Preheat the oven to 350°F/180°C. Lightly grease a 4-cup/1-liter shallow ovenproof dish with the butter.

2 Arrange a single layer of potato slices in the bottom of the prepared dish and top with half of the garlic, half of the sliced red onion, and one-third of the grated Swiss cheese. Season to taste with a little salt and pepper.

3 Repeat the layers in exactly the same order, finishing with a layer of potatoes topped with grated cheese.

4 Pour the heavy cream over the top of the potatoes and cook them in the oven for about 1½ hours, or until the potatoes are cooked through and the top is golden brown and crispy. Serve the potatoes immediately, straight from the dish.

herbed potatoes & onion

SERVES 4

4 large waxy potatoes, cut into cubes

heaping ½ cup butter

1 red onion, cut into 8 wedges

2 garlic cloves, crushed

1 tsp lemon juice

2 tbsp chopped thyme

salt and pepper

1 Cook the cubed potatoes in a pan of boiling water for 10 minutes, then drain thoroughly.

2 Melt the butter in a large, heavy skillet and add the red onion wedges, garlic, and lemon juice. Cook, stirring continuously, for 2–3 minutes.

3 Add the potatoes to the pan and mix well to coat in the butter mixture.

4 Reduce the heat, cover, and cook for 25–30 minutes, or until the potatoes are golden brown and tender.

5 Sprinkle the chopped thyme over the top of the potatoes and season to taste with salt and pepper. Transfer to a warm serving dish and serve immediately.

garlic mashed potatoes

SERVES 4

4 large mealy potatoes, cut into chunks

8 garlic cloves, crushed

¾ cup milk

6 tbsp butter

pinch of freshly grated nutmeg

salt and pepper

1 tbsp chopped fresh flat-leaf parsley, to garnish

1 Put the potatoes in a large pan. Add enough cold water to cover and a pinch of salt. Bring to a boil and cook for 10 minutes. Add the garlic and cook for an additional 10–15 minutes, until the potatoes are tender.

2 Drain the potatoes and garlic thoroughly, reserving 3 tablespoons of the cooking liquid.

3 Return the reserved liquid to the pan, add the milk, and bring to simmering point. Add the butter and return the potatoes and garlic to the pan. Mash thoroughly with a potato masher.

4 Season to taste with nutmeg and salt and pepper and beat the potato mixture with a wooden spoon until light and fluffy. Garnish with flat-leaf parsley and serve immediately.

spiced potatoes

SERVES 4

9 medium waxy potatoes

2 tbsp vegetable ghee

**1 tsp panch poran
spice mix**

3 tsp ground turmeric

2 tbsp tomato paste

1¼ cups plain yogurt

salt

**chopped fresh cilantro,
to garnish**

1 Preheat the oven to 350°F/180°C. Put the whole potatoes into a large pan of salted cold water. Bring to a boil, then simmer for about 15 minutes, until the potatoes are just cooked, but not tender.

2 Heat the ghee in a separate pan over medium heat and add the panch poran, turmeric, tomato paste, yogurt, and salt. Bring to a boil and simmer, uncovered, for 5 minutes.

3 Drain the potatoes and cut each one into 4 pieces. Add the potatoes to the pan, then cover and cook briefly. Transfer to an ovenproof casserole. Cook in the preheated oven for about 40 minutes, or until the potatoes are tender and the sauce has thickened a little. Sprinkle with chopped cilantro and serve immediately.

Step 1

Step 2

Step 3

pesto potatoes

SERVES 4

**2 lb/900 g small new
potatoes**

**3 cups fresh basil, plus
fresh sprigs to garnish**

2 tbsp pine nuts

3 garlic cloves, crushed

½ cup olive oil

**¾ cup mixed freshly
grated Parmesan-style
vegetarian cheese**

salt and pepper

1 Cook the potatoes in a pan of salted boiling water for 15 minutes, or until tender. Drain well, transfer to a warm serving dish, and keep warm until required.

2 Meanwhile, put the basil, pine nuts, garlic, and a little salt and pepper to taste in a food processor. Blend for 30 seconds, adding the oil gradually, until the mixture is smooth.

3 Remove the mixture from the food processor and place in a mixing bowl. Add the Parmesan-style vegetarian cheese and mix together.

4 Spoon the pesto sauce over the potatoes and mix well. Garnish with fresh basil sprigs and serve immediately.

mashed potatoes with cabbage

SERVES 4

heaping 2⅓ cups shredded green cabbage

5 tbsp milk

1½ cup diced mealy potatoes

1 large leek, chopped

pinch of grated nutmeg

1 tbsp butter, melted

salt and pepper

1 Cook the shredded cabbage in a pan of boiling salted water for 7–10 minutes. Drain thoroughly and set aside. Meanwhile, in a separate pan, bring the milk to a boil and add the potatoes and leek. Reduce the heat and simmer for 15–20 minutes, or until they are cooked through.

2 Stir in the grated nutmeg and thoroughly mash the potatoes and leek together. Add the drained cabbage to the mashed potato-and-leek mixture, season to taste with salt and pepper, and mix well.

3 Spoon the mixture into a warm serving dish, making a hollow in the center with the back of a spoon. Pour the melted butter into the hollow and serve immediately.

charbroiled vegetables

SERVES 6

2 sweet potatoes, sliced

3 zucchini, halved lengthwise

3 red bell peppers, seeded and cut into quarters

olive oil, for brushing

salt

salsa verde

2 fresh green chiles, halved and seeded

8 scallions, coarsely chopped

2 garlic cloves, coarsely chopped

1 tbsp capers

bunch of fresh parsley, coarsely chopped

grated rind and juice of 1 lime

4 tbsp lemon juice

6 tbsp olive oil

1 tbsp green Tabasco sauce

pepper

1 Cook the sweet potato slices in boiling water for 5 minutes. Drain and let cool. Sprinkle the zucchini with salt and let stand for 30 minutes. Rinse and pat dry with paper towels.

2 Meanwhile, make the salsa verde. Put the chiles, scallions, and garlic in a food processor and process briefly. Add the capers and parsley and blend until finely chopped. Transfer the mixture into a serving bowl.

3 Stir in the lime rind and juice, lemon juice, olive oil, and Tabasco. Season to taste with pepper, cover with plastic wrap, and chill in the refrigerator until required.

4 Brush the sweet potato slices, zucchini, and bell peppers with olive oil and spread out on a broiler rack or grill. Broil, turning once and brushing with more olive oil, for 8–10 minutes, until tender and lightly charred. Serve the vegetables immediately with the salsa verde.

couscous salad with roasted butternut squash

SERVES 4

2 tbsp honey

4 tbsp olive oil

1 butternut squash, peeled, seeded, and cut into ¾-inch/2-cm chunks

generous 1¼ cups couscous

1¾ cups low-salt vegetable stock

½ cucumber, diced

1 zucchini, diced

1 red bell pepper, seeded and diced

juice of ½ lemon

2 tbsp chopped fresh parsley

salt and pepper

1 Preheat the oven to 375°F/190°C. Mix half of the honey with 1 tablespoon of the oil in a large bowl, add the squash, and toss well to coat. Turn into a roasting pan and roast in the preheated oven for 30–40 minutes until soft and golden.

2 Meanwhile, put the couscous in a heatproof bowl. Heat the stock in a pan and pour over the couscous, cover, and let stand for 3 minutes. Add 1 tablespoon of the remaining oil and fork through, then stir in the diced cucumber, zucchini, and red bell pepper. Recover and keep warm.

3 Whisk the remaining honey and oil with the lemon juice in a pitcher and season to taste with salt and pepper. Stir the mixture through the couscous.

4 To serve, top the couscous with the roasted squash and sprinkle with the parsley.

Step 1

Step 2

Step 2

steamed vegetable parcels

SERVES 4

4 oz/115 g green beans

¾ cup sugar snap peas

12 baby carrots

8 pearl onions or shallots

12 baby turnips

8 radishes

4 thinly pared strips of lemon zest

4 tbsp unsalted butter or vegetarian margarine

4 tsp finely chopped fresh chervil

4 tbsp dry white wine

salt and pepper

1 Cut out 4 double thickness rounds of wax paper about 12 inches/30 cm in diameter.

2 Divide the green beans, sugar snap peas, carrots, onions, turnips, radishes and lemon zest among the rounds, placing them on one half. Season to taste with salt and pepper and dot with the butter. Sprinkle with the chervil and drizzle with the wine. Fold over the double layer of paper, twisting the edges together to seal.

3 Bring a large pan of water to a boil and place a steamer on top. Put the parcels in the steamer, cover tightly, and steam for 8–10 minutes, then remove the parcels from the steamer and serve them immediately, to be unwrapped at the table.

roasted vegetables

SERVES 4

1 onion, cut into wedges

2–4 garlic cloves, left whole but peeled

2¾ cups eggplant cubes

1 medium zucchini, trimmed and cut into chunks

10½ oz/300 g butternut squash, peeled, seeded, and cut into small wedges

2 assorted colored bell peppers, seeded and cut into chunks

2 tsp olive oil

1 tbsp shredded fresh basil

pepper

1 Preheat the oven to 400°F/200°C. Place the onion, garlic cloves, eggplant, zucchini, squash, and bell peppers in a large roasting pan, then pour over the oil. Turn the vegetables until they are lightly coated in the oil.

2 Roast the vegetables for 35–40 minutes, or until softened but not mushy. Turn the vegetables over occasionally during cooking.

3 Remove the vegetables from the oven, season with pepper to taste, and stir. Scatter with shredded basil and serve while still hot.

chinese vegetables

SERVES 4

2 tbsp peanut oil

4½ cups broccoli florets

1 tbsp chopped fresh ginger

2 onions, each cut into 8 pieces

3 celery stalks, sliced

6 oz/175 g young spinach

1½ cups sugar snap peas

6 scallions, quartered

2 garlic cloves, crushed

2 tbsp light soy sauce

2 tsp superfine sugar

2 tbsp dry sherry

1 tbsp hoisin sauce

⅔ cup vegetable stock

1 Heat the peanut oil in a preheated wok until it is almost smoking. Add the broccoli florets, chopped ginger, onions, and celery to the wok and cook for 1 minute.

2 Add the spinach, sugar snap peas, scallions, and garlic and cook for 3–4 minutes.

3 Mix together the soy sauce, superfine sugar, sherry, hoisin sauce, and vegetable stock. Pour the stock mixture into the wok, mixing thoroughly to coat all the vegetables. Cover the wok and cook over medium heat for 2–3 minutes, or until the vegetables are cooked through but still crisp.

4 Transfer the Chinese vegetables to a warm serving dish and serve immediately.

spicy bok choy with sesame sauce

SERVES 4

2 tsp peanut or vegetable oil

1 red chile, seeded and thinly sliced

1 garlic clove, thinly sliced

5 baby bok choy, quartered

scant ½ cup vegetable stock

sauce

2 tbsp sesame seeds

2 tbsp dark soy sauce

2 tsp light brown sugar

1 garlic clove, crushed

3 tbsp sesame oil

1 For the sesame sauce, toast the sesame seeds in a dry skillet over medium heat, stirring, until lightly browned. Remove from the heat and let cool slightly. Transfer to a mortar. Add the soy sauce, sugar, and crushed garlic and pound to a coarse paste with a pestle. Stir in the sesame oil.

2 Heat the peanut oil in a wok or large skillet. Add the chile and sliced garlic and stir-fry for 20–30 seconds. Add the bok choy and stir-fry for 5 minutes, adding the stock a little at a time to prevent sticking.

3 Transfer the bok choy to a warm dish, drizzle the sesame sauce over the top, and serve immediately.

Step 1

Step 2

Step 3

chinese-style gingered vegetables

SERVES 2

1 tbsp sunflower or peanut oil

1-inch/2.5-cm piece fresh ginger, peeled and grated

1 onion, thinly sliced

1 cup frozen green bean pieces

1 lb/450 g frozen mixed vegetables

⅔ cup water

2 heaping tbsp dark brown sugar

2 tbsp cornstarch

4 tbsp vinegar

4 tbsp soy sauce

1 tsp ground ginger

1 Heat the oil in a wok or large skillet, add the grated ginger, and sauté for 1 minute. Remove from the wok or skillet and drain on paper towels.

2 Reduce the heat slightly and add the vegetables and water to the wok.

3 Cover with a lid or foil and cook for 5–6 minutes, or until the vegetables are tender.

4 Mix the sugar, cornstarch, vinegar, soy sauce, and ground ginger together in a bowl. Increase the heat to medium and add the mixture to the vegetables in the wok. Simmer for 1 minute, stirring, until thickened.

5 Return the ginger to the wok and stir to mix well. Heat through for 2 minutes and then serve immediately.

mixed cabbage coleslaw

SERVES 4

3 oz/85 g red cabbage

3 oz/85 g white cabbage

2 oz/55 g green cabbage

1½ cups peeled and grated carrots

1 white onion, finely sliced

2 red apples, cored and chopped

4 tbsp orange juice

2 celery stalks, trimmed and finely sliced

2 oz/55 g canned corn kernels, drained

2 tbsp raisins

dressing

4 tbsp low-fat plain yogurt

1 tbsp chopped fresh parsley

pepper

1 Discard the outer leaves and hard central core from the cabbages and shred finely. Wash well in plenty of cold water and drain thoroughly.

2 Place the cabbages in a bowl and stir in the carrots and onion. Toss the apples in the orange juice, and add to the cabbages together with any remaining orange juice, and the celery, corn, and raisins. Mix well.

3 For the dressing, mix the yogurt, parsley, and pepper to taste in a bowl, then pour over the cabbage mixture. Stir and serve.

spiced lentils with spinach

SERVES 4–6

2 tbsp olive oil

1 large onion, finely chopped

1 large garlic clove, crushed

½ tbsp ground cumin

½ tsp ground ginger

generous 1 cup French green lentils

about 2½ cups vegetable stock

4 cups young spinach leaves

2 tbsp fresh mint leaves

1 tbsp fresh cilantro leaves

1 tbsp fresh flat-leaf parsley leaves

freshly squeezed lemon juice

salt and pepper

strips of lemon zest, to garnish

1 Heat the oil in a large skillet over medium heat. Add the onion and cook, stirring occasionally, for about 6 minutes. Stir in the garlic, cumin, and ginger and cook, stirring occasionally, until the onion starts to brown.

2 Stir in the lentils. Pour in enough stock to cover the lentils by 1 inch/2.5 cm and bring to a boil. Lower the heat and simmer for 20–30 minutes, until the lentils are tender.

3 Meanwhile, rinse the spinach leaves in several changes of cold water and shake dry. Finely chop the mint, cilantro leaves, and parsley.

4 If there isn't any stock left in the skillet, add a little extra. Add the spinach and stir through until it just wilts. Stir in the mint, cilantro, and parsley. Adjust the seasoning, adding lemon juice and salt and pepper. Transfer to a serving bowl and serve, garnished with lemon zest.

tomato rice

SERVES 4

1 onion, chopped

2⅓ cups peeled, seeded, and chopped plum tomatoes

1 cup vegetable stock

1 cup long-grain rice

salt and pepper

1 Put the onion and tomatoes in a food processor and process to a smooth puree. Scrape the puree into a pan, pour in the stock, and bring to a boil over medium heat, stirring occasionally.

2 Add the rice and stir once, then reduce the heat, cover, and simmer for 20–25 minutes, until all the liquid has been absorbed and the rice is tender. Season with salt and pepper to taste and serve immediately.

Step 1

Step 1

Step 2

crispy roasted asparagus

SERVES 4

16 asparagus stalks

2 tbsp extra virgin olive oil

1 tsp coarse sea salt

1 tbsp grated Parmesan-style vegetarian cheese, to serve

1 Preheat the oven to 400°F/200°C. Choose asparagus stalks of similar widths. Trim the bottom of the stalks so that all the stems are approximately the same length.

2 Arrange the asparagus in a single layer on a baking sheet. Drizzle with the olive oil and sprinkle with the salt.

3 Place the baking sheet in the oven and bake for 10–15 minutes, turning once. Remove from the oven, transfer to an attractive dish, and serve immediately, sprinkled with the grated cheese.

hot roasted bell peppers

SERVES 6

6 red bell peppers, seeded and cut into thick strips

½ cups seeded and thinly sliced, fresh green Serrano or jalapeño chile strips

2 garlic cloves, crushed

4 tbsp extra virgin olive oil

1 Preheat the oven to 400°F/200°C. Put the peppers, chiles, and garlic in a shallow casserole dish. Pour in the oil.

2 Cover and bake for 50–60 minutes, or until the peppers have softened. Remove the lid and reduce the temperature to 350°F/180°C. Return the casserole dish to the oven and bake for an additional 45 minutes, or until the peppers are very soft and beginning to char.

3 Serve immediately if serving hot. Alternatively, let cool, then transfer to a large screw-top jar and store in the refrigerator for up to 3 weeks, topped off with more olive oil to keep the peppers covered, if necessary.

lemon & garlic spinach

SERVES 4

4 tbsp olive oil

2 garlic cloves, thinly sliced

1 lb/450 g fresh spinach, torn or shredded

juice of ½ lemon

salt and pepper

1 Heat the olive oil in a large skillet over high heat. Add the garlic and spinach and cook, stirring continuously, until the spinach is softened. Be careful not to let the spinach burn.

2 Remove from the heat, turn into a serving bowl, and sprinkle with lemon juice. Season with salt and pepper. Mix well and serve either hot or at room temperature.

stir-fried broccoli

SERVES 4

2 tbsp vegetable oil

2 broccoli heads, cut into florets

2 tbsp soy sauce

1 tsp cornstarch

1 tbsp superfine sugar

1 tsp grated fresh ginger

1 garlic clove, crushed

pinch of dried red pepper flakes

1 tsp toasted sesame seeds, to garnish

1 Heat the oil in a large preheated wok or skillet over high heat until almost smoking. Add the broccoli and stir-fry for 4–5 minutes. Reduce the heat to medium.

2 Combine the soy sauce, cornstarch, sugar, ginger, garlic, and red pepper flakes in a small bowl. Add the mixture to the broccoli and cook, stirring continuously, for 2–3 minutes until the sauce thickens slightly.

3 Transfer to a warm serving dish, garnish with the sesame seeds, and serve immediately.

Step 1

Step 2

Step 2

lemon beans

SERVES 4

**2 lb/900 g mixed beans,
such as fava beans and
green beans**

5 tbsp butter or margarine

4 tsp all-purpose flour

1¼ cups vegetable stock

5 tbsp dry white wine

6 tbsp light cream

**3 tbsp chopped mixed
herbs**

grated zest of 1 lemon

2 tbsp lemon juice

salt and pepper

1 Cook the beans in a pan of boiling salted water for 10 minutes, or until tender. Drain and place in a warm serving dish.

2 Meanwhile, melt the butter in a pan. Add the flour and cook, stirring continuously, for 1 minute. Remove the pan from the heat and gradually stir in the stock and wine. Return the pan to the heat and bring to a boil, stirring.

3 Remove the pan from the heat once again and stir in the light cream, mixed herbs, and lemon zest and juice. Season to taste with salt and pepper. Pour the sauce over the beans, mixing well to coat thoroughly. Serve immediately.

peas with pearl onions

1 tbsp of unsalted butter

1 cup pearl onions

2 lb/900 g fresh peas, shelled

½ cup water

2 tbsp all-purpose flour

⅔ cup heavy cream

1 tbsp chopped fresh parsley

1 tbsp lemon juice

salt and pepper

1 Melt the butter in a large, heavy pan. Add the whole pearl onions and cook, stirring occasionally, for 5 minutes. Add the peas and cook, stirring continuously, for an additional 3 minutes, then add the measured water and bring to a boil. Lower the heat, partially cover, and simmer for 10 minutes.

2 Beat the flour into the cream. Remove the pan from the heat, stir in the cream mixture and parsley, and season to taste with salt and pepper.

3 Return the pan to the heat and cook, stirring gently but continuously, for about 3 minutes, until thickened.

4 Stir the lemon juice into the sauce and serve immediately.

red cabbage & beet slaw

SERVES 4

3¾ cups finely shredded red cabbage

1 cup julienned cooked beet

1 apple, cored and thinly sliced

1 tbsp lemon juice

1 tbsp sunflower seeds

1 tbsp pumpkin seeds

dressing

3 tbsp mayonnaise

2 tbsp Greek yogurt

1 tbsp red wine vinegar

salt and pepper

1 Put the cabbage, beet, and apple slices into a large bowl. Add the lemon juice and mix well.

2 To make the dressing, mix all of the dressing ingredients together in a separate bowl. Pour the dressing over the salad and stir well. Season with salt and pepper, cover, and chill in the refrigerator for at least 1 hour.

3 Stir the salad thoroughly and adjust the seasoning to taste. Sprinkle with the sunflower and pumpkin seeds just before serving.

spiced basmati rice

SERVES 4

scant 1¼ cups basmati rice

2 tbsp ghee, vegetable oil,
or peanut oil

5 green cardamom pods,
bruised

5 cloves

2 bay leaves

½ cinnamon stick

1 tsp fennel seeds

½ tsp black mustard seeds

2 cups water

1½ tsp salt, or to taste

2 tbsp chopped fresh
cilantro

salt and pepper

1 Rinse the rice in several changes of water, until the water runs clear, then let soak for 30 minutes. Drain and set aside until ready to cook.

2 Heat a casserole or large saucepan with a tight-fitting lid over medium–high heat, then add the ghee. Add the spices and stir for 30 seconds. Stir the rice into the casserole so the grains are coated with ghee. Stir in the water and salt and bring to a boil.

3 Reduce the heat to as low as possible and cover the casserole tightly. Simmer, without lifting the lid, for 8–10 minutes, until the grains are tender and all the liquid is absorbed.

4 Turn off the heat and use two forks to mix in the cilantro. Adjust the seasoning, if necessary. Recover the pan and let stand for 5 minutes.

VARIATION
For a bit of color and texture, finely chop some green beans or sugar snap peas and fry for a few minutes. Stir through the rice and serve.